1. VICTORIAN CLIFTON

Explore
Bristol

EXPL◉REWALKS UK

Julia Killingback and Michael Pascoe

The Downs

CLIFTON DOWN

	**Start**
	Victorian Clifton Walk
	slope
	Viewpoint
	Steps
••••	**Alternative Route**
	Meeting Point
🚌	**Bus Stop**
✠	**Church**
Taxi	**Taxi Rank**
☎	**Public Phone Box**
🚻	**Public Toilets**
	Children's Playground

The sea ←

RIVER AVON

THE PROMENADE

Mansion House

THE UPPER PROMENADE

Clifton Down

1. VICTORIAN CLIFTON

Explore
Bristol

ON FOOT

EXPL◉REWALKS UK

Observatory Hill

Suspension Bridge

0   100
Metres

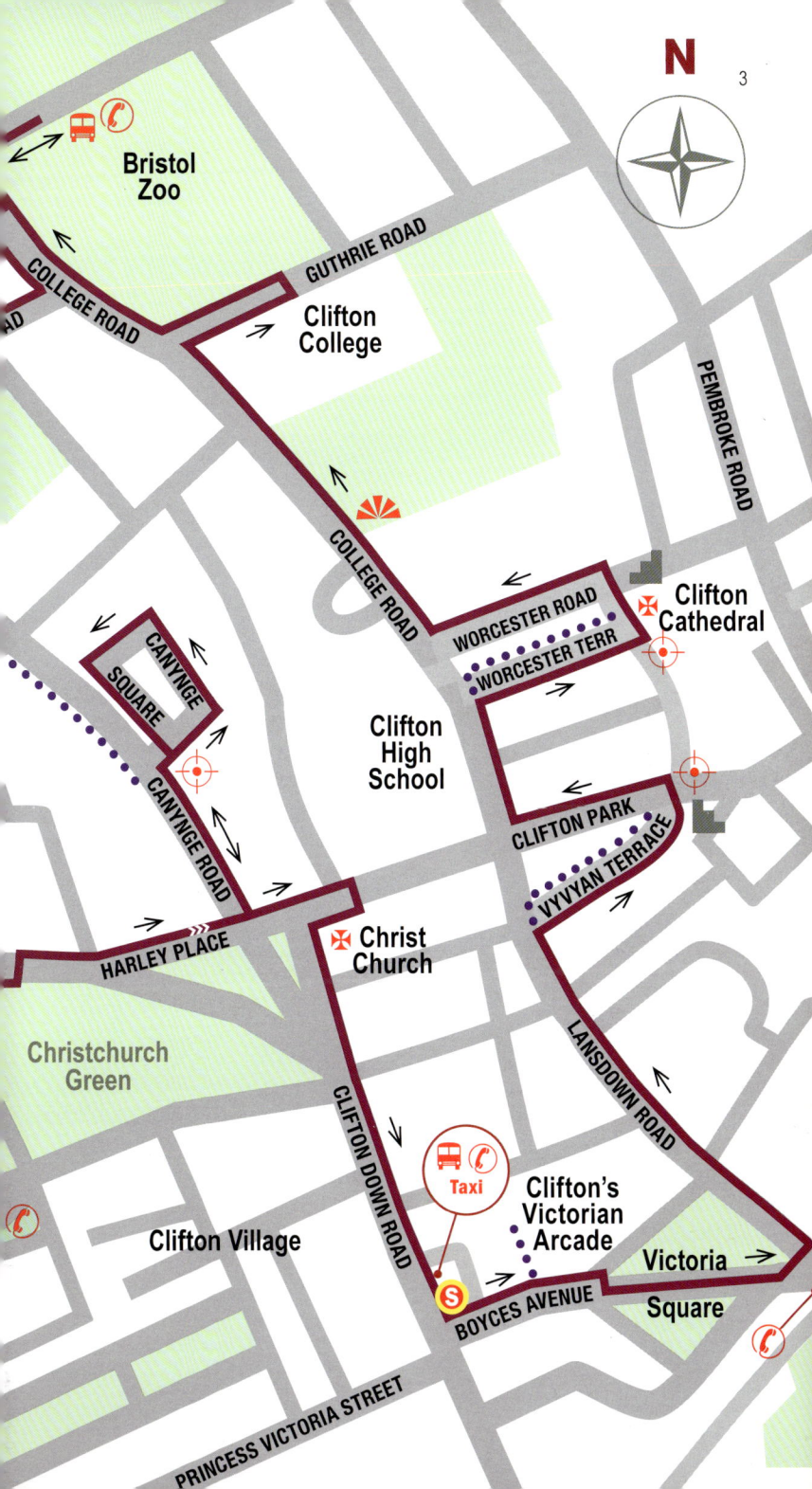

N

3

Bristol
Zoo

GUTHRIE ROAD

COLLEGE ROAD

Clifton
College

COLLEGE ROAD

PEMBROKE ROAD

WORCESTER ROAD

WORCESTER TERR

Clifton
Cathedral

CANYNGE
SQUARE

CANYNGE ROAD

Clifton
High
School

CLIFTON PARK

VYVYAN TERRACE

HARLEY PLACE

Christ
Church

Christchurch
Green

LANSDOWN ROAD

CLIFTON DOWN ROAD

Taxi

Clifton's
Victorian
Arcade

Victoria
Square

Clifton Village

BOYCES AVENUE

PRINCESS VICTORIA STREET

A Circular Walk around Victorian Clifton

The walk is mainly on the level, but alternative routes have been indicated where mobility is an issue.

Full Circular Walk
Total distance approx. 3³/₄ miles / 6.0 kms
Average time needed – 2 hours

Shortened Walk
Total distance approx. 2¼ miles / 3.6 kms
Average time needed – 1½ hours

Our walk description begins at the Clifton Village Bus Stop
See the map pages 2 and 3.
This stop is close to the junction of Boyce's Avenue with Clifton Down Road, near the pedestrian crossing.
OS Explorer map 154, Sat Nav: Postcode BS8 4AF

Get there
By bus – From Temple Meads Station
         – From Bristol City Centre
         – From Bristol Bus Station (a nearby stop)
Ask for the Clifton Village Bus Stop.

By Open Top Bus This makes a circular tour of Bristol (from February to December). It stops at the Clifton Village stop.
Seasonal information: www.citysightseeingbristol.co.uk

By taxi – ask to be set down near the Clifton Village Bus Stop.

Please note
This is a circular walk, so you may choose to begin at any point on our route knowing that you will return to the same spot eventually.

Mobility Impaired Information There are some steps and two slopes on this route. If you wish to avoid these, just look for our suggested **Options**. There are alternative routes marked on the map.

THE QUIZ When you see a numbered question in the text STOP!
Look for the question at the bottom of the page. You should be able to discover
the answer from this spot. When you think you know it, turn over– the numbered
answers are shown at the bottom of the NEXT page. GOOD LUCK!

😃 FUN FACTS. Look out for the smiley face telling you more as you go along.

🛝 There is a nearby children's playground. See map on page 2.

A Panorama of Clifton
Left – site of Victorian Clifton,
right – Georgian Clifton
*c.*1830 detail, Thomas Rowbotham

Welcome to Victorian Clifton

This walk takes you through Clifton as it developed during Queen Victoria's reign *(1837-1901)* but also describes some features from other eras as well. Bristol's important nineteenth-century industries of flour, chocolate, tobacco, printing, packaging and footwear flourished as well as the wine trade with its famous *Bristol Milk* and *Bristol Cream* sherries. Local coal mines and shipping both expanded greatly. The engineer Isambard Kingdom Brunel *(1806-1859)* built two ships in Bristol, first the *PS Great Western* and then the *SS Great Britain* which was launched in 1843 by Queen Victoria's consort, Prince Albert. Brunel also designed an amazing variety of structures, including the *Great Western Railway* which linked London and Bristol, as well as the famous *Clifton Suspension Bridge.* Find out more about the bridge in our Clifton walk.

After the Bristol Riots of 1831 Clifton on the hill was viewed as a safer and healthier area in which to live than the over-crowded city of Bristol below. These riots, which caused great destruction, were the worst outbreak of civil unrest anywhere in nineteenth-century Britain. (Brunel acted as a Special Constable during the disturbances.) They came about as the

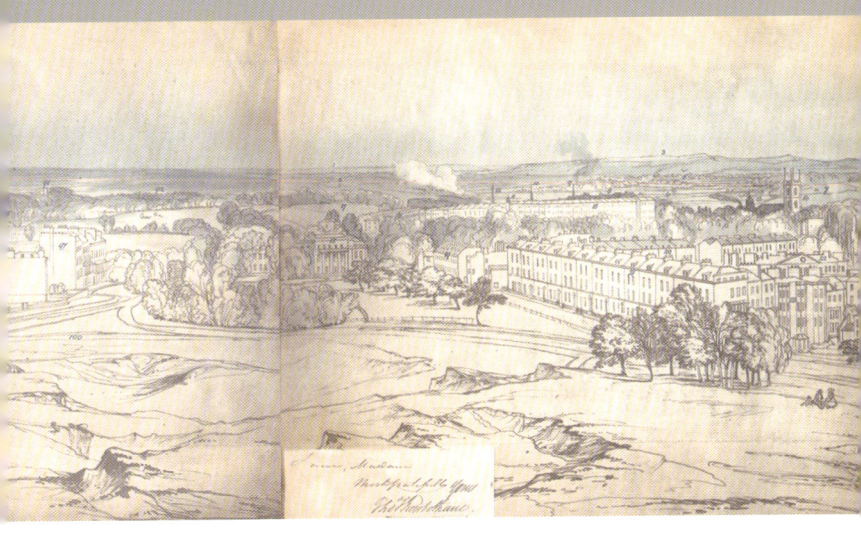

result of the demand by ordinary people for the right to vote, a right denied to many at that time, and contempt for the self-serving and corrupt City Council. The Reform Act of the following year increased the number of people allowed to vote, but many men, and all women, were forced to wait for a century for universal suffrage.

The nineteenth century saw the population of Clifton grow from 4,500 in 1800 to 28,000 by the end of the century. The area became home to rich merchants and industrialists as well as to the wealthy, professional, leisured and retired classes. They were looked after by an army of servants. Life, especially as a live-in servant, was far preferable to being a factory hand, a miner or a navvy and without today's mechanical domestic aids, human labour was necessary. Victorian tourists to Clifton rented lodgings in order to view Clifton's scenery, to visit the Suspension Bridge which had been opened in 1864, or to take the Hotwell spa waters.

With the arrival of a piped water system from a reservoir on the Downs and the building of a sewerage system in the middle of the century, bathrooms and lavatories were installed. Clifton became one of the healthiest places in the country in which to live.

▲ Aerial view of Clifton looking east

Towards the middle of the nineteenth century, the elegant, ordered Classical architectural style of the Georgian terraces fell out of fashion. The delicate look of the Georgian small-paned windows gave way to considerably larger panes following improved glass-making techniques. Substantial semi-detached villas and mansions in a variety of architectural styles, especially Gothic and Italianate, were built on former green fields to the north and east of Clifton Village. These were very spacious family houses, but today most are divided into flats.

The Society of Merchant Venturers, the association of Bristol's most important merchants, owned much of Clifton and acted as an early form

of planning authority. They insisted that new buildings erected on their land were to be of a high quality, and that ample green spaces were part of the plan.

The Merchant Venturers, owners of Clifton Down, promised in 1856 to maintain 'free and uninterrupted use of the Downs'. The City Council then bought commoners' rights on the adjoining Durdham Down. The two together then promoted the Downs Act of 1861 which allowed the Council to buy Durdham Down and thus preserved the Downs 'for ever hereafter', giving the citizens of Bristol 178 hectares (680 acres) of open common land. The Downs are jointly run by the Council and the Merchant Venturers.

Start facing the Clifton Village bus stop, close to the pedestrian crossing where **Boyce's Avenue** meets **Clifton Down Road**. Go left. Cross Boyce's Avenue. *Turn left towards the arch. Walk along, keeping to the right-hand pavement.* The shop fronts on your right below the tall building have fine Victorian decorative detail. *Stop to look at King's Road on your left.* It is remarkable for its carved stone decoration and the unusual brick banding dating from Victorian times. *Continue.*

➔ On your left is the entrance to the Moorish-influenced *Clifton Arcade*, a wonderful example of a Victorian shopping mall, built in 1878. Early on it failed commercially, was used as a furniture store for a hundred years, and happily was restored for shopping in 1992. The original shop fronts remain. Look at the rose window at the far end. It looks real. It's not. It's painted. Perhaps after your walk you will return to enjoy this fascinating arcade.

😊 The buildings around the cobbled courtyard opposite were stables for Georgian *Boyce's Buildings* nearby. In Victorian times the yard would have been busy with horse-drawn carriages coming and going. Imagine a horse being saddled up for you to gallop across the Downs!

● **Question 1** *(Look at the bottom of the page).* The shop under the arch has a Victorian façade and an original brass doorstep – Victorians took a great pride in their polished brass (left). Look through the shop window to see the painted plants and creatures on the walls and ceiling.

➔ Go under the arch past the old wrought-iron gate into **Victoria Square**. Stop close to the arch. Look at *Albert Lodge* on your left, a fine Classical detached villa named after Queen Victoria's husband. It was built in the 1840s.

● **Question 1**
What can you see carved in stone over the arch?

● **Question 2**
What animals guard the coat of arms?

TURN OVER FOR ANSWERS

There is some clipped shrub topiary in the garden, a popular feature in Victorian times. The Square was developed at three separate dates and its three sides are all different from one another. The fourth side was never built as a terrace but as a series of large villas. The terrace on your left, close to you, *Royal Promenade*, was the second side, built in 1851. Look along the buildings with their substantial stone balconies and heavy railings.

The nearby row at right angles to this was the last to be built and was completed in 1874. Close by you, at Number 15, is a plaque to Dr W. G. Grace *(1848-1915)* the great England and Gloucestershire cricketer, who lived here from 1894-1906. The cast-iron railings show a variety of handsome designs. Originally the Square's gardens were designed as one open space, now they are divided.

➡ Take the diagonal footpath across the square. Look up to your left to the middle of *Royal Promenade* and you will see Queen Victoria's coat of arms carved in stone.
⬤ **Question 2**

🔺 **Royal Promenade**
Completed *c.*1851
Thomas Foster & Son
Architects

🔺 **Victoria Square**

The finest suburb in England
Sir John Betjeman *(1906-1984)*

Imagine the gardens in Victorian times, enjoyed exclusively by the householders living around the Square. Their key allowed access to the then completely railed off gardens. The general public was restricted to the diagonal path. With its high railings and metal arches overhead, no wonder that it was nick-named Birdcage Walk! Walk on. The railings were removed during the Second World War *(1939-1945)* to help the war effort and never replaced.

When the garden was designed some unusual trees were planted, but only a few of these, the largest and oldest in Bristol, now remain. They include the very fine Cedar of Lebanon, in the middle of the lawn to your left, and two Beeches, (one copper and one Cut-leaf) close to the path, all dating from the 1840s. The last tree on the left is an Italian Maple, one of only two in Bristol. Beyond it on the left, overhanging the wall, close to the road, is an old Mulberry tree, leaning almost horizontally.

🙂 The square's Victorian children must have had fun playing in these then very private gardens! Look either side of the path towards the main road. The dips in the ground here hide a long forgotten route that once linked the two. Imagine them playing chase through a tunnel that went right under the path you are standing on!

➔ Leaving the gardens, turn left. Cross the pedestrian route towards the last right-hand house of **Lansdown Place**. This terrace was the first side of Victoria Square to be built in 1845. Now walk left along it. Unusually, the pillars supporting the railings are made of cast iron. There are fine balconies and scrolls either side of the doors.

🙂 Victorian families living here had servants below stairs to help them. Some children may have been allowed to visit the lofty basement kitchens to watch cook making a Steamed Suet Pudding. *Mmmm!*

Answer 1
The head of young Queen Victoria. This stone carving is like her picture on the first-ever postage stamps and the early coins of her reign. See "Private Collections"

Answer 2
A lion and a unicorn with its single horn. You won't meet a real unicorn. They are imaginary beasts!

Like their predecessors, the Georgians, Victorian cooking for the rich was done by servants in the basements, although these rooms were often higher and better lit than kitchens in earlier houses. Continue along.

At Number 13 is a plaque to Dr William Budd. He realised as early as 1847 that typhoid and cholera were caused by polluted water, not poor air as had been generally believed. As a result Bristol's water supplies were enormously improved. Look across at *Royal Promenade*. The end house bears its name carved in stone.

The spire ahead of you is that of *Christ Church* which you will see later. Cross the end of Kensington Place and continue along **Lansdown Road**. Look at the charming corner turret with its coronet on the last house at the end of Mortimer Road to your left.

→ Walk on, leaving *Christchurch Primary School* to your right. Look at the terrace of five houses on the other side of the road with stained-glass above the front doors and ground floor windows. Walk on.

▲ **Lansdown Place**
Built 1835
Attributed to Foster & Son
Architects

Do you remember this song?
Here we go round the mulberry bush,
The mulberry bush,
The mulberry bush.
Here we go round the mulberry bush
On a cold and frosty morning.

→ **Cross the end of Royal Park and Vyvyan Road, both on your right.** Having just passed Manilla Road, to your left, pause to look back at the extraordinary mix of decorative terracotta mouldings on the houses. It is Victorian details like these that Sir John Betjeman *(1906-1984)* the poet, writer and admirer of Clifton, brought to the attention of the general public.

You now pass *The Bristol School of Dancing,* known as *The Studio.* It was built in 1893 as a Swedish Gymnasium. Exercise apparatus, ropes and rhythmic dancing were all the rage at the time. In the early 1920s the building was acquired by the prima ballerina Miss Phyllis Bedels who founded the *West of England Academy of Dancing* and then went on to establish an *Association of Operatic Dancing* which, in 1935, became the world-renowned *Royal Academy of Dancing* in London. Dance, both traditional and modern, is still taught here today.

😊 What kind of dancing do you like?

The two bas-relief plaques were created by the Danish sculptor Bertel Thorvaldsen *(1770-1844).* He was regarded as the Rodin of the north and was extremely popular and successful, specialising in classical figures. The plaque on the right represents *Night.* She carries two babies, *Sleep and Death,* and a night owl hovers beside them.

Just beyond there is a garden gate with a cast-iron grille.
● **Question 3**

→ **Continue until you reach Vyvyan Terrace on your right.** Stop at this end to admire the impressive view along it.
If you prefer to avoid the steps at the far end, cross the road to the pavement opposite. Walk parallel to the gardens. The Meeting Point is at the far end at the base of the steps.

The terrace was completed in 1847 and named after a local Member of Parliament. It was designed to look like a palace.

● **Question 3**
Look carefully!
What is the bird having
for his lunch?

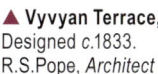

Walk along the wide pavement to appreciate the handsome façade of this imposing building. It demonstrates a rich variety of styles – different columns, elegant balconies, fine stone balustrades and original ironwork. This really is urban planning on a grand scale! The fanlights over the doors no longer resemble the fan-shaped ones that shed light into Georgian hallways. Number 2 has its original Victorian letterbox – too small now to easily receive today's bulky mail, but once, no doubt the perfect size for a hand-written billet-doux.

The terrace has its own private garden in front of it. You will see a Cedar tree and, at the far end of the garden, a Weeping Silver Lime, the finest in Bristol. Both are from the original Victorian planting.

▲ **Vyvyan Terrace,** Designed *c.*1833. R.S.Pope, *Architect*

 Reaching the end of the terrace, walk down the steps.

 **Meeting Point**

Mathematics

The style of the columns in the centre of the terrace is *Greek Ionic* – one of the so-called *Orders* of Classical architecture. The height of a *Greek Ionic* column is generally 9 times the diameter of the base, so you don't have to take a ladder with you to work out its height.

→ Cross the main road and turn left. You are now in **Clifton Park**. Walk on, leaving Vyvyan Terrace gardens on your left.

You will pass several large villas which date from the 1830s. Number 9 has elegant pillars to support the gates and complex pierced stone balustrades.

Number 8 has a magnificent Copper Beech and an ingenious iron runner to guide the two gates, one for pedestrians, the other for horse-drawn vehicles. ●**Question 4**

→ Walk on to the corner. Now cross the top of **College Road** and turn right along it. Walk a few paces and look across the road at the impressive house. It dates from 1832. The name of the house, *Leny*, is carved on the shield over the door. As you walk past look back again at the house. ●**Question 5**

→ Walk on. You will pass Cobblestone Mews, originally the stables and coach houses for Clifton Park and Worcester Terrace. The cobbles are original, all hand-cut, and the street is one of very few streets in Clifton still lit by gas.

🙂 In Victorian times a lamplighter went around the streets at dusk with a taper and a long ladder lighting lamps. He returned at dawn to put them out.

The Lamplighter
W. H. Pyne 1805

To your left are the entrance gates to *Clifton High School*, an independent school. The main building at the far end is rather hidden beyond a huge Copper Beech planted in 1850. The school, originally for girls, was founded in 1877 by Dr John Percival *(1834-1918)*, Headmaster of nearby Clifton College. Percival's daughter, Bessie, in later years referred to her time there as *a dream of delight*.

→ Cross College Road to imposing classical **Worcester Terrace**. **Stop here to read on**.

The terrace dates from 1853, and like *Vyvyan Terrace*, has its own private garden in front of it. It was named after the Marquess of Worcester *(1824-1899)* the eldest son of the Duke of Beaufort. (The family still retain their estate at Badminton, near Bristol, home of the famous horse trials.) It

Clifton High School

Answer 3
Figs and a snail!

● **Question 4**
What is unusual about the stone gatepost of Number 7?

● **Question 5**
Here's a challenge. What words are painted on the side of this grand covered entrance?

was designed by Charles Underwood and was one of the last of Clifton's grand, palace-like terraces. Note the detail of the crinoline balconies, the stone rosettes above the doors and windows and the ironwork. There are steps at the far end. The building seen beyond the trees is a Cathedral.

➔ Walk along the terrace.

> If you have difficulty managing steps,
> walk along the road parallel to the raised pavement
> to the base of the steps leading up to the Cathedral.
> ⊕ This is the Meeting Point.

The last house on the right, beyond the terrace, Number 12, has a fine entrance with Ionic columns to its portico. Cross the road to the wide rear entrance steps of the Cathedral.

▲ **Worcester Terrace**
Built *c.*1848-53
Charles Underwood
Architect

Did you know?
In the 1850s the latest fashion for wealthy ladies was the ornate and ample crinoline dress. They had to manage their vast skirts with care. This style of "crinoline' balcony would have helped.

This is the Roman Catholic *Cathedral of Saints Peter and Paul*, consecrated in 1973, one of the earliest to be built in concrete. Far removed from the architecture of Victorian times, this is an award-winning building. You may enter the cathedral – visitors are welcome. If you wish to see inside the cathedral, use this entrance.

It was the first cathedral to be built after the Second Vatican Council of the 1960s which encouraged congregations to be grouped around the altar so that they should feel, and be part of, the celebration of the Mass. Inside, the cathedral has a huge uninterrupted communal space, with flexible seating for 900, and starkly decorated walls which soar up to the central tower. The colourful stained glass windows are by Henry Haig. *The Way of the Cross* is illustrated by fourteen low-relief sculptures in concrete designed and executed by William Mitchell. The selected events are based upon the Biblical accounts of the Passion of Christ.

● **Question 6** (*inside the cathedral*)

➡ Leave the Cathedral by the same door, making your way back to the wide steps. Now turn right to cross **Worcester Road** (which runs along the side of the Cathedral).

➡ Turn left. Walk back to College Road, leaving Worcester Terrace gardens to your left.

😊 Look out for the first older house here. A stone carver has decorated it with flowers and fruits that look good enough to eat!

It was expensive to move stone long distances so that many Clifton houses were built by digging out the foundations which provided both building stone and a cellar. Some of the Avon Gorge stone was naturally red, stained with iron, and this is often seen on Clifton buildings, contrasting with pale yellow Bath stone, frequently used for corners and window surrounds.

Answer 4

The house name *Fairlinch*, its number, 7 and the street name, Clifton Park are carved in stone.

Answer 5

'Conflict tests the warrior'.

Note the red and purple roof tiles and the stylish pierced terracotta ridge tiles on the houses. Stop at the gate of the final house here. ● **Question 7**

➔ Joining **College Road** again, turn right, keeping right.

▲ **The Baptistry Window R C Cathedral** Consecrated 1973 Stained Glass by Henry Haig

In 1877, at Number 8, the first trial of a telephone in Bristol took place – from one part of the house to another! Shortly after, Alexander Graham Bell *(1847-1922)* inventor of the telephone, demonstrated to 600 Bristolians at the City Museum that *they could hold a friendly conversation... and even flirtation carried on.* One of his patriotic staff positioned in a shop over the road, sang *God Save the Queen* down the line to the Lady Mayoress!

Note the old wall to your right. No expense was spared – it was not unusual for a garden wall to have decorative banding in the Victorian period. Walk on.

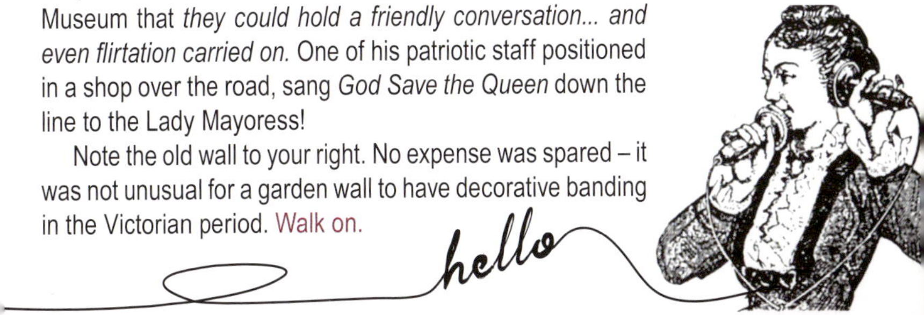

● **Question 6**
Look at the font. Doves are flying around it.
How many are there?
Count them quietly.

● **Question 7**
Which animal guards the door of Number 1?

➜ *You arrive at a small driveway leading to your right. What a view! Stop to enjoy it and then read on.* You will see the magnificent façade of *Clifton College,* an independent school, across the well-kept playing fields. Close by you there is a plaque to the poet Henry Newbolt *(1862-1938)* who was educated here. He made these playing fields, known as *The Close,* famous by writing a poem which typifies the Victorian virtues of service and loyalty, with the well-known lines *Play up, play up and play the game.* Newbolt would still recognise the site as it is today.

The school was designed by Charles Hansom *(1817-1888)* the brother of the inventor of the Hansom Cab, and opened in 1862. The various buildings were built successively from 1860 onwards and are a remarkable example of Victorian Gothic architecture – a total contrast to the Classical Vyvyan and Worcester Terraces.

To your right, beyond *The Close,* you can see the aluminium spire of *All Saints Church*, consecrated in 1868. The church was bombed during the Second World War and in 1967, when it was rebuilt, a flêche was placed on what remained of the original tower. The square tower, well to its left, is all that remains of the blitzed *Emmanuel Church* of 1865, now a home for the elderly. The crime novelist Agatha Christie was married to an army officer here on Christmas Eve 1914.

To its left is the *School Chapel* with its hexagonal copper-clad lantern. This was created when the building was enlarged in 1910. Left of this again, the earlier narrow bell tower was built in 1862, before the chapel. The sound of the bell ringing out over *The Close* is familiar to many generations of staff, pupils and local residents. A large blue and gold-faced clock that marks the hours of the school day hangs on the bell tower wall. Left of this is the steeply-gabled main school hall – known as *Big School* – the oldest College building.

➜ Walk along College Road beside the playing fields.

Answer 6
There are six – three flying upwards and three swooping down! Doves are said to be the birds of peace.

Answer 7
A lion. Look too for the heads of a king and queen who also decorate the front of the house.

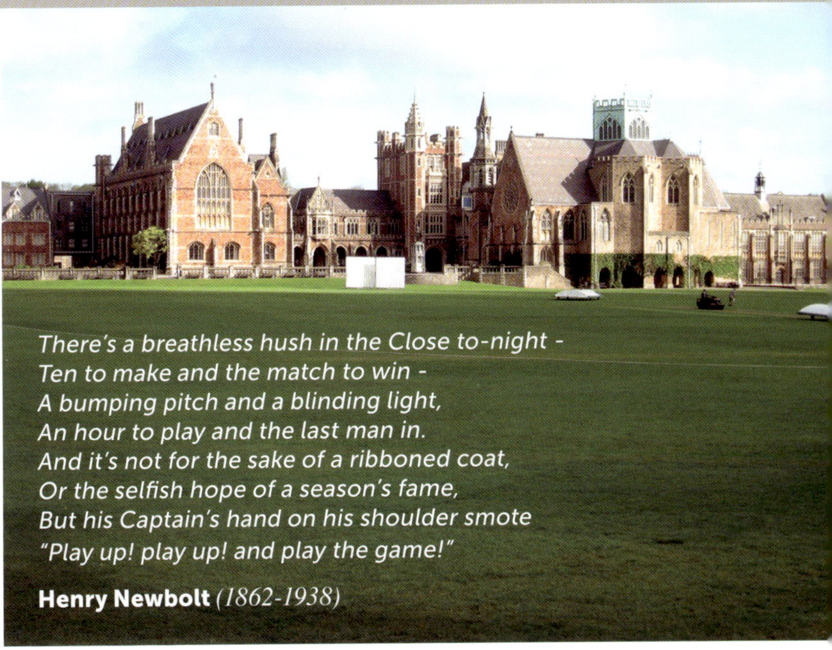

> *There's a breathless hush in the Close to-night –*
> *Ten to make and the match to win –*
> *A bumping pitch and a blinding light,*
> *An hour to play and the last man in.*
> *And it's not for the sake of a ribboned coat,*
> *Or the selfish hope of a season's fame,*
> *But his Captain's hand on his shoulder smote*
> *"Play up! play up! and play the game!"*
>
> **Henry Newbolt** *(1862-1938)*

The Lime trees on the edge of *The Close* were planted in 1862.

▲ **Clifton College**
Built 1860
Charles Hansom, *Architect*

🙂 Imagine a boy of twelve stepping out on to this pitch to play cricket in 1899. A.E.J.Collins (right) made the highest score ever recorded- 628 runs, not out – it's still a record. *Well played, that man!*

Collins did not live long enough to see how his record would endure. Like so many of his fellow-pupils, the newly-married young man was killed in 1914 in the carnage of the First World War *(1914-1918)*.

On the other side of the road there is a series of large semi-detached villas dating from the 1870s. Numbers 20 and 22, *The Cloisters*, have typical Victorian Bath stone details. The garden walls have retained their original carved stone balustrades. At the end of *The Close* look back at the cricket pavilion which was built in 1922. Continue along.

Although cricket rules were laid down as early as 1774, it was not until Victorian times that the game became popular with players and spectators alike.
W. G. Grace (1848-1915), England's most famous cricketer, coached the team at nearby Clifton High School when his daughter was a pupil there.

Oakeleys House

School Hall

Look left at the decorative woodwork used on the school's boarding houses. You will now reach the main school entrance. This fine *Memorial Arch* is dedicated to the 853 former boys and masters who fell in the two World Wars *(1914-1918)* and *(1939-1945)* and whose names are inscribed within it. The Latin inscription above the arch is the school motto and roughly translates as *The spirit grows within.*

The *Memorial Arch* was designed by Charles Holden *(1875-1960)* who was also the architect of Bristol Central Library; Bristol Royal Infirmary's King Edward VII Building; University College London, Senate House; London Transport HQ and many underground stations. The arch was dedicated in 1923. It was Holden's only Gothic-style building.

Field-Marshal Sir Douglas Haig *(1861-1928)* (left) attended the dedication. Haig was a former pupil and later became Commander-in-Chief of the British and Imperial armed forces in the First World War. You can glimpse his statue by William McMillan RA *(1887-1977)* on a plinth to the left inside the school grounds.

A more recent former pupil is the actor John Cleese, *(born 1939)* star of the *Monty Python* and *Fawlty Towers* television series, and of many films.

Through the archway there is a fine view of the *School Chapel* with its large rose window. To its left is the huge *School Hall.* ● **Question 8**

Opposite the school gateway, across the road, are more school boarding houses with typical Victorian bargeboards beneath their gables.

➔ Walking on, you reach *School House*, the corner building on your right. This was the earliest boarding house and the home of the first headmaster, John Percival *(1834-1918)*, who was appointed when he was only 28. Under his leadership the school grew from just 76 to 600 boys in fifteen years.

You will arrive at the corner of **Guthrie Road**. ● **Question 9**

● **Question 8**

Look up at the roof. What creature carries a flag with CC (Clifton College) cut into it?

● **Question 9**

Look up at another roof across the road. What creature can you see?

➡ **Turn right and walk along the right-hand pavement of Guthrie Road.** The second building across the road is the Clifton College *Music School*. It has fine gates. ● **Question 10** The flag on the tower shows the date of the building. On the school building, *Watson's House*, to your right, you can see a little further on a pair of griffins on the stonework of the bay window.

😃 Something else is happening here. Guess why these two naughty schoolboys are slithering down the stonework. Do you think that they are in trouble for forgetting to do their homework?

Just beyond, on the following building, even the drainpipes are decorated. As you walk along you will see lions and gargoyles on the buildings to your right.

▲ **Memorial Arch**
Clifton College
Built 1923
Charles Holden, *Architect*

Details from the Music School gates

● **Question 10**

There are two stone carvings of musical instruments. Can you name them?

Look up at the lofty school tower. During the Second World War pupils were sent away from Bristol to safer places. The school was then taken over by American Forces, planning the invasion of Europe. A radio receiver was installed at the top of the tower and linked to code-breakers at *Bletchley Park*. Intelligence about the enemy was radioed to the American generals here. As the top room was approached by a spiral staircase, total security was achieved by having a Marine sentry, bayonet fixed, at the bottom of the stair. The school still flies the stars and stripes every 4th July, American Independence Day. Cross the road to the rear gates of *Bristol Zoo*.

 The elephants on the gate have a message for us!

The huge creatures called Ying and Yang crawling around on the other side are the work of Julian Warren, a local sculptor in metal. ● **Question 11** Now, retrace your steps but on the right-hand pavement. Pause at the far end.

Across the road, outside the classrooms of the *Coulson Centre*, is a very rare tree. This was planted about thirty years ago by a College Headmaster's wife. It's called a Scholars' Tree! Go right beside the zoo wall passing Cecil Road.

You pass the *Clifton Pavilion* with its fine Art Deco canopy over the entrance. Walk on to the corner. You have reached the road called **Clifton Down**. The vast space of open parkland beyond it is known as *The Downs*. This common land, grazed by sheep for centuries, now belongs to the citizens of Bristol. Foxes and deer are occasionally seen.

➜ Now turn right towards the distinctive Zoo gates which date from its opening in 1836. ● **Question 12**

When the Zoo was established this was open countryside, well outside the city of Bristol. Isambard Kingdom Brunel *(1806-1859),* designer of the *Clifton Suspension Bridge*, was one of the first subscribers.

Answer 8
A griffin, (it's a pretend animal, half lion and half eagle).

Answer 9
A cockerel made of copper which has oxidised.

Answer 10
A harp, cymbals, and horn on one side. A lyre, trumpet and pan-pipes on the other

Bristol Zoo has played an important role in the development of British zoos. Johnny Morris, the broadcaster, introduced children to animals here in his television programmes in the 1950s and the writer Gerald Durrell collected animals for it. In the past the Zoo housed many more large animals, the most famous of which was the greatly-loved Alfred, a gorilla, who can now be seen preserved in the *Bristol City Museum*.

The Zoo has always been known for its beautiful gardens and has a magnificent tree collection, although most of the original Victorian tree planting has had to be replaced in recent years. Today it concentrates on animal breeding, education and global conservation. If you have time (and you will need plenty) it is well worth a visit.

➡ Leaving the zoo, return to **College Road**. Cross using the pedestrian crossing. Look out for more animals decorating the gate. Then pause to look up left at the Pavilion roof with its turret. ● **Question13**

▲ **Bristol Zoological Gardens**
Opened 1836

▼ **Entrance lodges to Bristol Zoo** c 1909

● **Question 11**
What huge creatures appear to be crawling around on the other side of the gates?

● **Question 12**
Look!
The animals are parading across the entrance!
Can you name them?

● **Question 13**
What animal can you see keeping watch over the Zoo?

→ Reaching **Cecil Road** turn right. There is a Balsam Poplar tree on the corner opposite. Cecil Road is a row of fine semi-detached Italianate villas, dating from the 1860s, pleasantly set back behind front gardens. These were family houses where, without today's modern conveniences, servants would have been employed to keep the household running efficiently.

Wealthy Victorian parents were often very strict. Children were expected to be seen and not heard. The smallest were watched over by nursery maids at the top of the house. Before girls' schools were established most older girls were taught at home by governesses while older boys were sent away to public schools.

→ Stay on the right-hand pavement and continue along it. You will pass a road called College Fields to your left. This borders the *New Fields,* another sports ground for Clifton College, first played on in 1884. There is a fine decorated cast-iron lamp standard and very close to it, in the garden wall to your right, are some particularly rough stones at different levels. Look closer! ●**Question 14** The wall belongs to *Auburn House,* perhaps given this name because of the red stone used in its construction. (The adjacent area to Clifton is called *Redland*, no doubt because of the local stone.) Look at the fine example of a Victorian porch.

▲ Auburn House

→ Stop at the junction with Clifton Down by the post box. From here you can see, on the opposite corner, usually with a flag flying, a large Victorian house. During the Bristol Riots of 1831 the original Mayor's mansion in the heart of Bristol was destroyed. In 1867 Alderman Thomas Proctor *(1812-1876)* bequeathed this house to the city as the *Mansion House.* In 1899 Queen Victoria decreed that Bristol should henceforth have a *Lord* Mayor, elected by councillors. In 2011 Bristol's citizens were given the opportunity to elect a Mayor. Mayor George Ferguson was voted into office.

Answer 11
Two larger-than-life stag beetles. Thank goodness they aren't real!

Answer 12
From left to right: elephant, apes, ostrich, hippopotamus, giraffe, rhinoceros, bison, eland, bears, deer, giraffe, lynx, monkey, camel, lion, tiger, kangaroo and an elephant.

➜ Cross Cecil Road, then **Canynge Road**, to walk towards the *Mansion House* gates. You can see a typical Victorian conservatory filled with plants. The Victorians were great collectors of newly imported, often exotic plants. A little further along you will come to the grand stone entrance gates carved with delicate swags, castles and ships. Look below the lamp on the central section of the wall. You will see the Bristol coat of arms. ● **Question 15**

Beyond is a Wellingtonia tree and the imposing canopied entrance to the Mansion House now used for both civic and private events.

➜ The walk continues and is full of interest including a beautiful Victorian tree-lined promenade. There is a moderate slope in this next section described on page 29.

▲ **The Mansion House**
Built *c.*1867
George and Henry Godwin
Architects

Answer 13
A lion, known as the king of all beasts. Which way is the wind blowing today?

● **Question 14**
What can you see?

● **Question 15**
Look at the shield. What things are on it?

Option – For those unable to manage the slope, there is a more level route described below which will re-join the circular walk later – see the map on pages 2 and 3.

➡ From the gates of the *Mansion House*, continue along the same pavement (Canynge Road) leaving Clifton College's playing field to your left. You will cross the end of Litfield Road. The small houses here were once coach houses.

To your right are semi-detached Victorian villas in various styles. At Number 47 note the use of contrasting coloured stone and floral carving. The low wall has the remnants of Victorian railings, removed like many others during the Second World War to provide metal for armaments.

➡ Walk on to Percival Road. Cross it and pause on the opposite corner. Look diagonally across at a pair of male and female Honey Locust trees, the oldest in Bristol. The female tree carries clusters of seed pods.

➡ Continue along **Canynge Road** towards a large gate. You will see a plaque dedicated to Ellen Sharples *(1764-1849)* and her daughter Rolinda *(1793-1838)* local artists, (below left), who once lived at Number 37, Canynge Road. Ellen Sharples outlived her daughter and donated over £5,000 for the establishment of a Fine Art Academy. This opened in 1858 and has now become the highly-regarded Royal West of England Academy of Art in Queen's Road, Clifton.

On your left you can see the façades of the fine houses in Canynge Square. You pass beneath the branches of a magnificent Copper Beech tree growing in the garden of Number 33, Norland House, built about 1820.

➡ Once you reach the bend in the road, cross it to the entrance of **Canynge Square** (right-hand pavement).

⊕ **Meeting Point**

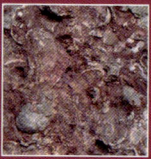

Answer 14
Fossil sea shells. How amazing to think that these creatures lived on a warm sea bed millions of years ago.

Answer 15
A ship on the sea. A castle on a cliff. Unicorns hold the shield and a soldier's helmet.

Continuing the circular walk.

➜ Make your way back to the post box on the corner of Cecil Road and Clifton Down where you were earlier. Pause.

With your back to the Clifton Down road sign and the lamp post on your left, you will see some Birch trees opposite the Mansion House. The larger tree to the right of the first Birch is the rarest tree in Clifton, a Cluster Oak, one of only six in the whole country.

➜ Now walk along **Clifton Down**. Keep the huge detached villas of the 1850s to your right. The first of the houses in the row is *Sutton House*, (now unnamed), the last is *Tellisford House*.

➜ Pass the gate of *Tellisford House*, and turn the corner to get a clearer view of its complex stonework and curved Dutch gables. No wonder it was once described as *frantic Jacobean*.

▲ **Tellisford House**
Built *c.*1855
Henry Goodridge, *Architect*

The Proctor's Fountain

You are now at the top of Bridge Valley Road, where there used to be a turnpike. The road drops down to the tidal River Avon, 92 metres/300 feet below. With your back to the gate of *Tellisford House* you can see a Gothic-style fountain re-sited on the Green nearby.

➜ Cross the road and take the path to the fountain.

Like the nearby *Mansion House*, the fountain was given to the city by Alderman Proctor in 1862. It commemorates the gift of the Downs to the citizens of Bristol by the Merchant Venturers. Pleased with his fountain, Proctor wrote, *Ordinarily, the three cups attached to the fountain are sufficient; but to meet any extra demand my man* [servant] *takes out a number of half-pint mugs and turns on an extra supply of water.* The Bristol Water Company charged him 1 shilling (5p) per 1,000 gallons (4,500 litres).

➜ Return to the main road, towards the bus stop. Cross the road to the beautiful avenue of Beech trees on the far side. This is called *The Promenade,* and was created in 1826, perhaps copying the Mall in London. It is at its most beautiful in the early spring and again when the leaves turn gold in the autumn.

Straight ahead of you, under a large oak tree close to the road junction, there is a green plaque. The tree was planted in 1903 to celebrate the coronation of Queen Victoria's eldest son, King Edward VII *(1841-1910)* the previous year.

😊 Sundays for wealthy children could be dull. A long church service was followed by a formal family luncheon. Thank goodness on fine days they could walk with their parents on the Promenade, perhaps meeting friends and listening to the popular music of the day being played on the bandstand that was there then.

➜ Walk on under the archway of branches. Look out for the large mansion on your left, near the bend in the road. It is distinguished by a huge Copper Beech in the driveway.

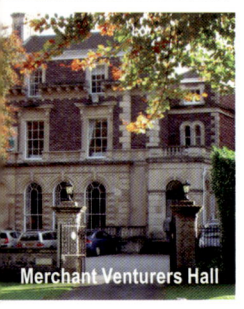
Merchant Venturers Hall

The turnpike

Did you know?

During the mid-eighteenth century turnpikes were privately owned. Tolls collected were needed to maintain the roads. Tolls varied for different types of horse-drawn vehicles and even herds of sheep and cattle. Turnpikes declined with the advent of the railways.

This is the *Merchant Venturers' Hall*, the headquarters of Bristol's ancient association of merchants, bearing their splendid coat of arms. In 1832 the Society was involved in setting up the Great Western Railway Company. It also played a leading role in the creation of Clifton and Durdham Downs and the Clifton Suspension Bridge. The Society moved here in 1945 after the destruction of their sixteenth-century hall in the city during the 1940 Blitz.

➔ Continue along. The path now begins to rise. Look out for *Trafalgar House* c.1830-35, with its fine columns.

😊 Victorian gardeners were keen to collect seeds from exotic countries. One of these grew into this huge Monkey Puzzle tree with its spikey evergreen branches. It would take a brave monkey to climb it!

➔ Continue up the slope on the same path, the Upper Promenade.

▲ **The Promenade**
Laid out in 1826 as the grand road into Clifton from the turnpike

Did you know?
The motto of the Society of Merchant Venturers is:
Indocilis Pauperiem Pati
One who cannot learn to endure poverty – Horace (65-8BC).

Engineers House

Iron Age Dobunni coin

The last house, before Percival Road, has a splendid Cedar tree. After the junction with Percival Road you will see *Engineers' House* (formerly Camp House). This was the home of Mayor Charles Pinney during the Bristol Riots of 1831. The destruction down in the city caused richer people to move uphill to live here in the relative safety of Clifton. Walk on up the slope. Ahead of you to the right of the path you will see some embankments – traces of the outer ramparts of an Iron Age Hill Fort of about 350 BC. This lofty, once pallisaded fort would have provided a perfect lookout across the Avon Gorge, to the Mendip Hills and northwards to Wales. It was later used by the Romans as a military camp. ➜ Continue along.

At the bend, the road name below you changes to **Litfield Place**. You pass *Dorset House*, built in 1825, formally the Royal Marines Reserve Headquarters.

➜ *Christchurch Green* now opens out before you. At Observatory Road cross towards the footpaths opposite. Take the smaller one, on the left. It runs closest to the main road in the direction of the church. Look left. House numbers 3 and 2 Litfield Place have beautiful ornate ironwork.

➜ Walk on. Look out for a very small path joining from the right. Once here, cross the main road to *Litfield House* opposite.
● **Question 16** Look at the railings with their Egyptian-inspired lotus flowers. The curved motifs towards the top of the gate pillars are also in the Egyptian style. Thirty years before this house was built, the French Emperor Napoleon had invaded Egypt. Although Britain was at war with France at that time, all things Egyptian became very fashionable.

➜ Go right, cross the top of steep Camp Road to **Harley Place**. Opposite, on the edge of the Green, there is a Georgian milestone which says *To Bristol 2* (miles).

   The ugly block of 1960s flats here show a lack of sensitive planning at the time. Walk along the lower pavement. The terrace of Harley Place (detail left) was begun in the 1780s but not completed until about 1820. Look for number 9.

● **Question 16**
Look carefully at the front of the house. Can you say who built it and when?

What's in a name?
Litfield is derived from lead field. Lead was quarried here in the sixteenth century.

▲ **Harley Place**
Built *c.*1790
William Paty, *Architect*

Georgian streets were dark at night so householders, like those at Number 9, were made to put a lighted candle above their doors which shed light inside and out on to the street. It wasn't until much later that gas street lights, then electric ones were invented.

The ironwork on Number 8 includes an original mounting for a gas light of the early nineteenth century. It also has a pretty fanlight above the front door.

During both Georgian and Victorian times coal was necessary as fuel for the stoves so that servants could cook, for heating water, and to supply the individual fires in each room. After Number 4 you will pass some iron plates in the pavement which are the covers to the original coal holes. Coalmen arrived by horse and cart and tipped their sacks of coal into the cellars below. Stop at the corner.

Did you know?

Bristol had coal mines. Most productive were Kingswood, dating from Roman times, and Bedminster, begun in 1745. In Victorian times coal was delivered up the hill by horse and cart. No wonder it was particularly expensive in Clifton! The mines closed in the 1920s but their tunnels still exist.

➜ Cross the road and turn left down it, staying on the right-hand side. The road is named after a medieval Bristol merchant and shipowner William Canynge. You pass a small-scale Georgian terrace dating from the 1830s.

In Victorian times richer ladies wore crinoline dresses. Their skirts were made to look huge by a large cage of metal or whalebone which was sewn into an underskirt. How did these fashionable ladies squeeze up and down their narrow staircases? In these houses the stairs are just 68 cm/27 ins wide. Easy! The cages were bendy and could be neatly folded closely around the ladies when necessary.

The last house of the terrace, which has a modern entrance, bears a plaque to Conwy Lloyd Morgan *(1852-1936),* first Vice-Chancellor of the University of Bristol and pioneer of experimental psychology. Walk on down.

There is an attractive Victorian terrace on your left dating from 1870. The enclosed front gardens with their neat uniform walls and gate posts still exist exactly as they were meant to be. (In many cases Clifton house owners have removed these features to provide car parking, so destroying much of the charm of this historic area.) Note the well-restored stone decoration at Number 17 – opposite the entrance to the modern office block. You now reach **Canynge Square**.

⊕ **Meeting Point**

➜ Turn into the Square. It is actually a triangle consisting of three terraces – a series of delightful houses surrounding a pleasant garden. It was completed in the 1850s. Unusually, it is still lit by gas lamps. Walk anti-clockwise round the square. See at Number 8 a plaque to Samuel Jackson *(1794-1869)* one of the Bristol School of Artists who flourished in the early nineteenth century. At Number 20 Jeremy Rees (1937-2003) founder of *Arnolfini,* Bristol's dockside gallery of modern art, is commemorated.

Samuel Jackson

Answer 16

Charles Dyer, Architect in 1830 – the name and date are carved into the stonework on the right side of the portico. Dyer designed many important buildings in Bristol and London including the nearby Victoria Rooms, used by the Victorians for dances and concerts.

There is an original Victorian lamp bracket and lamp outside Number 33. The author E H Young *(1880-1949)* wrote several novels about Clifton including *Chatterton Square* which was based on Canynge Square. ●**Question 17**

➜ Now retrace your steps back to *Christchurch Green.* Turn left and walk along. The corner house was a farmhouse in the seventeenth century. The following century a new façade was added. The surrounding land, where you have been walking, was open farmland right up to the nineteenth century. (See the panorama on page 6.)

▲ **Canynge Square**
Completed 1850

 Guess what! Where Christ Church now stands ducks once swam happily on their pond.

The plaque on the third house along, Penrose Cottage, is dedicated to the poet and essayist, Walter Savage Landor *(1775-1864)* who once lived here. He was notorious for his bad temper and is reputed to have thrown his cook out of the window on to a bed of violets! ●**Question 18**

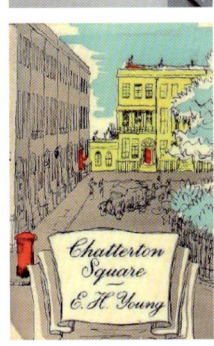

●**Question 17**

Look at the tree opposite No 41. It has an unusual name. Guess what?

●**Question 18**

Look up.
Do you know what the badge on the wall is for?

➜ Continue. You will pass two plaques. The first commemorates the birthplace of Sir Fabian Ware *(1869-1949)* the founder of the Commonwealth War Graves Commission which cares for the Allied War Cemeteries worldwide. The next is dedicated to Sir Archibald Russell (1904-1995) a distinguished Bristol aero engineer and aircraft designer.

➜ Cross Clifton Park Road and then Clifton Park via the pedestrian refuge to Victorian *Christ Church*, Clifton's parish church. Follow the pavement around to the porch. Pause here.

In the nineteenth century the population of Clifton grew rapidly. Victorians moving into the area had large families and servants so the then current parish church of St Andrew's (see our Clifton walk) was no longer adequate. Charles Dyer (1794-1848) was therefore commissioned to design Christ Church. It opened in 1841 and the spire was added later in 1857.

😊 Look up at the tall spire! When it was nearly finished, lots of people came to watch. A workman put the final round stone on the top. All of a sudden, he amazed the crowd by standing on his head on it! Everyone gasped and clapped and he climbed down to pass his hat around to collect money. Now there is a cockerel weather-vane on top. Do you think that at night he flies away to the North, the South, the East and the West?

Christ Church welcomes visitors.

➜ Leaving the porch, walk towards the mini round-about beyond Christchurch Road. To your right, on Christchurch Green, you will see a tall obelisk dedicated to Prime Minister William Pitt the Elder *(1708-78)*. Closer to you stands one of the oldest war memorials in the country, with an urn on top of it. This commemorates those officers who fell in India and the Philippines during the Seven Years War *(1756-63)*

Answer 17

A Handkerchief Tree. Atishoo! It flowers in spring and its unusual handkerchief-shaped flowers look like washing hanging out to dry. The Victorians discovered these trees in China and brought them to England. It is sometimes known as the Dove Tree.

against France and Spain. It has an interesting inscription noting the British tradition of chivalry. Both monuments were erected by General Sir William Draper *(1721-1787)* who conquered the Philippines. They originally stood in the nearby grounds of his now demolished mansion, *Manilla Hall,* named after the capital of the Philippines. When the Hall later became a convent the nuns insisted that these symbols of war and politics should be removed from their garden.

▲ **The War Memorial and Obelisk** on Christchurch Green

Answer 18

Today, the Fire Service will put a fire out. In Victorian times, householders couldn't get help unless they had paid money to a Fire Insurance company. The badge (a fire mark) on the front of a house showed that they had paid. This one is for the Liverpool, London & Globe Insurance Company and has the date 1836. Just think, fire engines were then pulled by galloping horses!

To the right of the mini-roundabout stands a large former Victorian *Congregational Chapel*. It was opened in 1868 and was intended as a rival building to *Christ Church*. A spire was to be built but funds ran out. It is now used partly as offices and also for sheltered housing.

➜ Cross the top of Manilla Road. You are now on **Clifton Down Road**.

On the opposite corner are the much older *Rodney Cottages*. In the seventeenth century these were originally two-up, two-down farm labourers' cottages. Like many such buildings their owners extended them in Georgian times and gave them a then fashionable new façade.

➜ Continue along Clifton Down Road.

You will pass on your left three of Clifton's earliest mansions. These were built in the second half of the eighteenth century by successful merchants and gentlefolk who wished for a country house. This area was countryside then but near enough to the city to be convenient for their businesses. The next large mansions to be built after these were those you saw close to the *Promenade* featured on this walk.

Freemantle House

➜ Pause by magnificent *Freemantle House.* This was the home of Abraham Isaac Elton of the Elton family of Clevedon Court. ● **Question 19**.

➜ Pass *Duncan House* and cross Mortimer Road. Next is *Mortimer House*. In the mid-1700s Edward Mortimer's daughter Mary married neighbour Abraham Elton's son, Isaac – a convenient courtship between two wealthy families.

Admiral Rodney

➜ Pause here to read about Rodney Place opposite.

It was built in about 1789 and named after Admiral Rodney *(1718-1792)*. The *Cottages*, former *Lodge* and *Place* are all named after this most successful of seamen. Amongst other endeavours he defeated the French fleet at the Battle of the Saintes in 1782, ending their threat to Jamaica. A grateful

Elton.

● **Question 19**
Look for a gap in the hedge – peep through. Watch out children! There's a fierce animal lurking there.
What is it?

nation created him Baron Rodney and, as Bristol merchants had many interests in Jamaica and the West Indies, the Admiral was made a Freeman of the City.

Number 2 was the home of Paule Vezelay (1892-1984). Born in Bristol as Marjorie Watson Williams, she was educated at nearby Clifton High School. She joined the avant garde set in France (hence her change of name). She exhibited at the Tate Gallery, London, becoming Britain's first acclaimed abstract artist. (See right an example of her early work.)

Other residents include Dr Thomas Beddoes *(1760-1808)* who lived at Number 3 as did his pupil John George Lambton (1792-1840) who later became the Earl of Durham and eventually Governor-General of Canada. Two magnificent trees in the gardens are a Plane and a Copper Beech.

→ Cross Kings Road and you will arrive at the Clifton Village bus stop where your walk began.

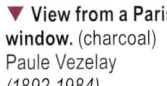

▲ **Rodney Place** *c.*1789
Joseph Fussell, *Builder*

▼ **View from a Paris window.** (charcoal)
Paule Vezelay
(1892-1984)

Maybe it's time to give yourself a well-deserved treat in one of Clifton's many cafés. In Victorian times such treats were reserved for the wealthy, but all Victorians enjoyed a good cup of tea. You might wish to go back to the delightful *Arcade* in close-by Boyce's Avenue to browse at your leisure.

As you visit the Arcade shops it is not difficult to imagine finely-attired Victorian gentlemen with their elaborately-dressed wives perusing the latest goods. Their strictly-disciplined children, with their noses pressed against the toyshop windows, would have wondered if they dare ask if they could have the new wooden spinning top or that pretty doll dressed in a silken crinoline.

Meanwhile, Mr Isambard Kingdom Brunel would have been hurrying past with his head buzzing with measurements for his new Suspension Bridge. How sad he didn't live to see completion of his first daring project which he touchingly called

My first child, my darling.

▶ **Portrait of I. K. Brunel**
by John Calcott Horsley *(1817-1903)*

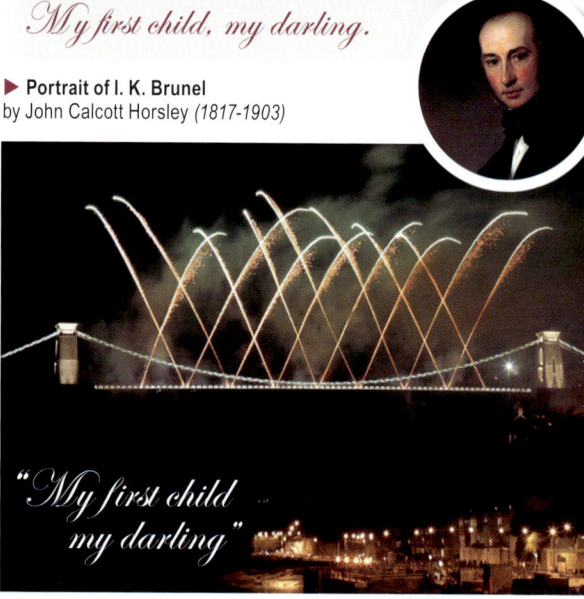

"My first child my darling"

▲ **Detail from a woodcut**
by Arthur Boyd Houghton
(1836-1875)

Answer 19
It's a lion...
ROAR!
But he hasn't got
his eye on you!

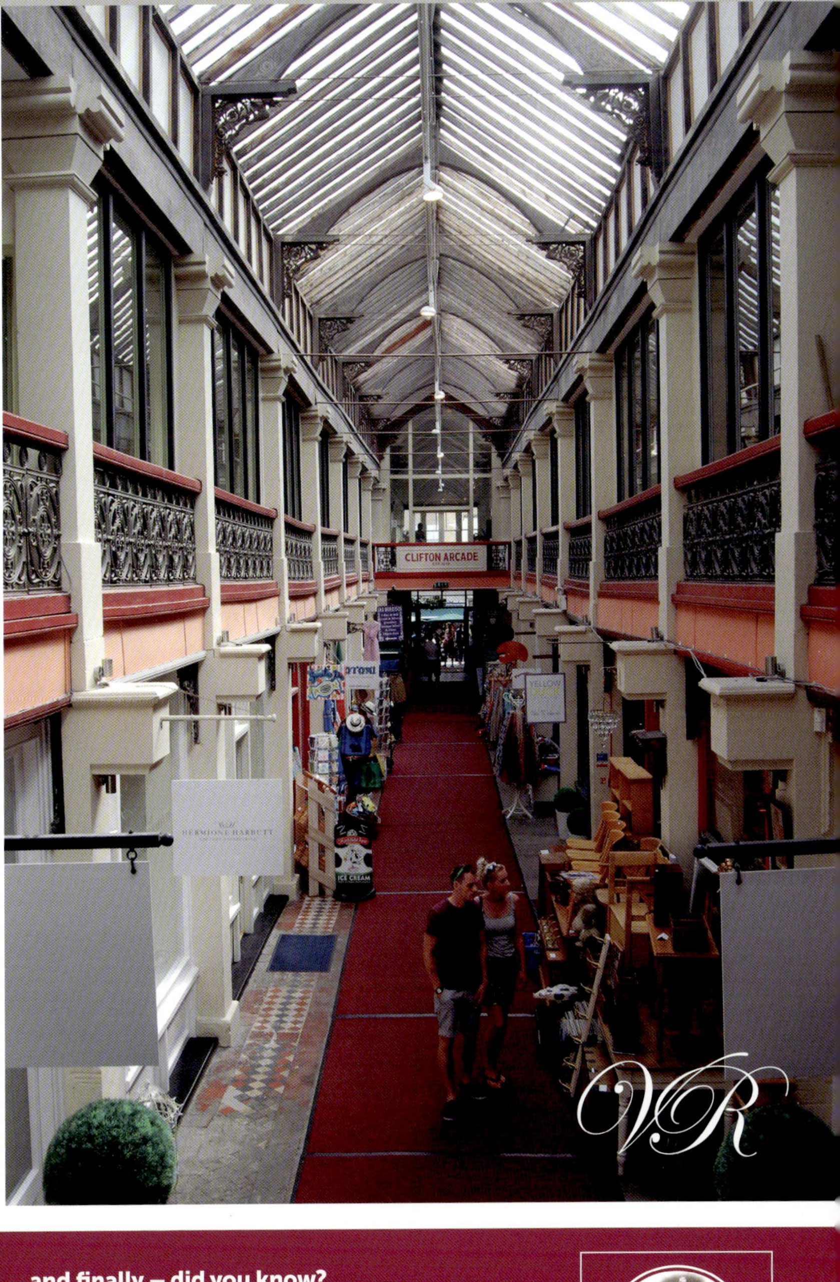

Photograph by Simon Bishop

... and finally – did you know?

Queen Victoria once allegedly said 'We are not amused', but we hope you were amused by this Victorian Clifton walk.

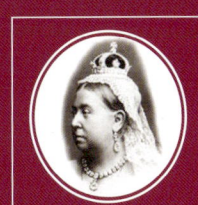

The Authors

Julia Killingback

A long-term resident who has been much involved in projects promoting this beautiful area. Julia studied art in Bristol (NDD ATD) designing dress textiles in Paris before returning to Bristol to establish her own Studio. Her designs were used on varied products by well-known companies worldwide. Previous published work. Illustrations for 7 Littlest Poetry Books. Author and Illustrator of 12 children's books (Methuen).

Michael Pascoe

Michael Pascoe has made a DVD - "Clifton - a place for all seasons" produced by 1st-Take and a book "The Clifton Guide" published by Redcliffe Press as well as writing many articles on Clifton and Hotwells' rich history. More recently, he co-authored the official guide to the Clifton Suspension Bridge. In 2005 he was awarded the Lord Mayor's medal "for services to Bristol and Clifton".

Acknowledgements:

The authors are most grateful for the goodwill and generosity of the following in helping towards the preparation of this book:

Pippa Gibbs for her kind and attentive editing; Simon Bishop for his expertise in graphic design; Richard Bland's assistance with the flora and fauna and Dawn Dyer (Bristol City Reference Library) for her unfailing help.

Our thanks also go to Anthony Beeson, Simon Gibbs, Francis Greenacre, Elvyn Griffiths, Clara Hudson, Andy Lillie, Tom Mocek, RoseMary Musgrave and Pim Palmen.

The authors would especially like to thank the friends and the families who kindly 'route tested' our walks in all winds and weathers – and approved them! Their comments were invaluable.

Credits

The authors and publishers are most grateful for permission to reproduce the following Illustrations which are © copyright of the organisations or individuals listed:

Key

(PC) = Postcard
(CNU) = Catalogue Number unknown
L = Left – from top down, then base panel L-R
R = Right – from top down, then base panel L-R

Illustrations reproduced by kind permission of the following:

Bristol Central Reference Library (BCRL)
P12L1, L4; P14L2, L4; P16L2; P18L4-P19R2; P26L1, L4; P33R2; P33 R3; P34L2; P38L4; P40L1; P41R2

Copyright Bristol City Museums, Galleries and Archives (BMAG)
P6-7; P28L4(CNU); P34 4(CNU)

Clifton College
P20L2; P21R2; P21R3 detail from P20L2

Clifton High School
P39R2

The Clifton Suspension Bridge Trust P8-9; P40(Mid Page), P41R2

The Random House Group Ltd
P35R3

From Private collections
P5L-R (5)
P10L3 JK; P12L5; P 38L5 JK (Elton Mayo Archive)

Julia Killingback (Illustrations)
P13 R3; P 16L4; P24 L4; P25 R2; P30 L4; P32 L2; P35 R4; P36 L3

Front & inside front cover
Simon Bishop

Back cover
Clifton Promenade Evening 1878
Bristol Illustrated Magazine (Unsigned)
MP Private Collection

Back cover image of Bristol Mayor George Ferguson
© The Post www.thisisbristol.co.uk

Wallace & Gromit's Grand Appeal
Bristol Children's Hospital Charity Donate
(www.grandappeal.org.uk/donate)

Every effort has been made to trace and acknowledge the source of all illustrations included. We should like to apologise for any errors or omissions.

Organisations

www.themerchantventurers.org; www.bristolzoo.org.uk; www.cliftononline.net; www.cliftonvillagetraders.org; The Clifton and Hotwells Improvement Society

Photographs

Most photographs were taken by Julia Killingback and Trevor Palmer. Our thanks are due to Trevor, also to James Barke, and Simon Bishop.

All images are copyright of the photographers unless otherwise stated.

Useful web addresses

Bristol Central Library:
www.bristol.gov.uk/libraries

Bristol City Museums and Art Galleries:
www.bristol.co.uk/museumsandgalleries

Clifton and Hotwells Improvement Society:
www.cliftonhotwells.org.uk

Bus information:
www.firstgroup.com/ukbus/bristol_bath

Tourist Information:
www.visitbristol.co.uk

Open Top Bus:
www.citysightseeingbristol.co.uk
Enquiries 07425 788123

Support funding for this project was kindly provided by Bristol City Council Neighbourhood Partnership Well Being Fund

All information is correct at the time of going to press. The authors cannot be held liable for any changes which may have occurred subsequently.

Text copyright © 2013 Julia Killingback and Michael Pascoe.

Series design concept and drawn illustrations
© 2013 Julia Killingback

First published 2013 by Julia Killingback Explorewalks UK
All rights reserved.

Printed by Short Run Press, Exeter
ISBN 978-1-906477-99-8

EXPL◉REWALKS UK
An imprint of Tangent Books
Web orders:
www.explorewalks.co.uk

For our families with love – and for all who delight in taking a step out of the ordinary
JK & MP

Explore
Bristol

EXPL◉REWALKS UK

Other Explorewalks titles in this series.

No 1. Clifton
2013

No 3. Cliftonwood
2014

No 4. Hotwells
2014

For information on other walks guides in this series go to

www.explorewalks.co.uk